The god of the Church Growth Movement

Martin Murphy

Second Edition

The god of the Church Growth Movement

Copyright © 1996 by Martin Murphy

Published by: Theocentric Publishing Group
1069A Main Street
Chipley, Florida 32428

http://www.theocentricpublishing.com

Library of Congress Control Number: 2016918161

ISBN 9780986405587

Preface

The church growth movement has fascinated me since my days as a student at Columbia International University formally known as Columbia Bible College and Seminary. It is the kind of concept that leaves you charmed by its frills, thrills, and entertainment. It has captured the attention of churchmen around the world. "Marketing the church" has replaced the biblical concept of "making disciples." The Mega-church has replaced the biblical concept of a shepherd and the flock. Some church growth movement entrepreneurs believe that the day of the churched culture is over. It is important to realize that the church growth movement finds its most faithful followers referring to "contemporary worship" or talking about the "emerging church." These recent inventions spring forth from the church growth movement. My inquiry into the mechanics of the church growth movement began years ago and I continue to trace its development. This book is the result of my observation, research, and inquiry into the church growth movement. This is my critique of the movement and I have published another book that presents a biblical model for church growth, *The Church: First Thirty Years*.

My purpose in the first part of this book is to explain how modernity is inseparably related to the church growth movement. Although this work includes a brief explanation of modernity, the primary focus is on the church growth movement, which is found in the last half of the book.

I hope Christians everywhere will take a serious look at the Christian landscape and ask the question: Has truth lost its savor in the church, particularly the evangelical church? Has the modern evangelical church moved from truth to compromise, confusion and contradiction? I argue that it has; so what will we leave the next generation? Will it be the wood, hay, and straw of the church growth movement or will it be the gold, silver, and precious stones of God's eternal truth?

Table of Contents

1. The Church

"When I am violently beset with worldly thoughts, for a relief, to think of death, and the doleful circumstances of it."[1] The pressure of secularism seems to have pressed against the soul of Jonathan Edwards at a time when worldliness and secularism were despised by the Puritans. However, the relationship between the secular and the sacred has a long history of discussion. During the time Jonathan Edwards lived the term *worldly* was popular, but it had the same meaning as secularism. Dr. John Gerstner made the wise observation that "Many have interpreted the Half-way Covenant as a breakdown of strict Puritanism as New England business began to give birth to prosperity and with it greater secularism."[2]

It is too ambitious to blame the problems that cause trouble for the evangelical church on this present age. The accumulation of problems started with the birth of the evangelical church in the 16th century.

The term *evangelical church* will be used in this discussion to describe classical evangelicalism. The theological distinctions of the Protestant Reformation are by Scripture alone, by faith alone, and by grace alone. They were also recognized by the early reformers as marks of the evangelical church. The evangelical church in the 16th century could have been called the Protestant church or the Reformed church. The Protestant church of the 16th century was interested in the truth of the gospel. For instance, the Roman Catholic Church taught, justification by faith. It may sound like good biblical doctrine but the Roman Catholic Church had lost the biblical understanding of justification. The Reformers corrected the misunderstanding of justification by adding, by faith alone. What has happened to the church that restored theological integrity to the gospel? The evangelical church "has cheerfully plunged into astounding theological illiteracy"[3] leaving behind the *only* that made them distinctively evangelical. The true evangelical church has diminished as those distinctive doctrines that set the evangelical church apart in the 16th century have been largely abandoned by professing evangelicals.

The collapse of the evangelical church may be attributed to any number of factors. It is not the purpose of this study to trace the decline of the evangelical church. However, the evangelical church has certainly been affected by modernity and the church growth movement. The argument set forth is that although modernity has shaped the character of the evangelical church, the church growth movement is the driving force to implement the tools of modernity in the evangelical church.

Since the church is central to the Christian religion I must say a few words about the church. Let me begin by quoting a theologian who was ahead of his time.

> The church has almost dwindled down into a secular corporation; and the principles of this world, a mere

carnal policy, which we have nick-named prudence, presides in our councils. Until she becomes a spiritual body, and aims at spiritual ends by appointed means, and makes faith in God the impulsive cause of her efforts, our Zion can never arise and shine, and become a joy and a praise in the whole earth. (James H. Thornwell, February 7, 1842)

If he was alive today he would probably say more critical things about the church. I hope this brief overview will help people think before they use the word church in any way that denigrates the true meaning of the body of Christ.

The church is not singularly identified. It is embodied within two dimensions commonly known as the visible church and the invisible church. The church visible is mixed with wheat and tares. One prominent church creed describes the visible church as the whole "number of professing Christians, with their children, associated together for divine worship and godly living, agreeable to the Scriptures and submitting to the lawful government of Christ's kingdom." The church invisible is the church in heaven. The invisible church is the true church or to put it another way the saved church. The invisible church is infallible, indestructible, indivisible, and universal.

A question that few people ask and fewer can answer is, "What is the church?" The evidence that few understand the biblical meaning of the word *church* may be found in expressions like, "come visit our church this Sunday," or "we have church every Sunday morning," et al. The notion that Christians "have church" or "go to church" shows the gross misunderstanding of the biblical doctrine. The church goes to worship or to put it another way the church assembles to worship. To understand what the church is, it is necessary to understand the nature of the church, the purpose of the church, the mission of the church, and the ministry of the church.

How much analysis have Christians given toward examining the nature of the church? What is the church or more precisely what is the nature of the church? We find the church mentioned throughout the New Testament. For instance, in Matthew chapter sixteen the Lord Jesus says, "I will build my church" (Matthew 16:18).

The Bible does not have a specific proof text to prove the nature of the church. The full counsel of God must be consulted to discover the nature of the church. The Bible does use metaphors that describe the nature of the church. A metaphor is a figure of speech that draws a comparison between two things. The comparison is not literally expressed and may be understood by implication. Although space does not permit inquiry into all the biblical metaphors a few of them will suffice.

The first metaphor I bring to your attention is the vineyard (Matthew 21:33-46; John 15:1-8). The nature of the vineyard is such that it is productive. Likewise the church is productive when it fulfills the responsibilities given to the church according to the Word of God. The preaching of the Word of

God has been given to the church. When the church insures the sound preaching of the Word of God, it is productive.

The field is another metaphor that will help us understand the nature of the church. The field belongs to God; the church is the field, therefore God's people belong to Him (1 Corinthians 3:5-9).

The Bible also uses another agricultural metaphor to describe the nature of the church. That metaphor found often in the gospel of John is a flock (John 10:1-16). Raising sheep was common in all ancient Near Eastern cultures. Sheep provided food, clothing, and sacrifices for religious worship. Sheep need a shepherd to tend to them and protect them. The sheep/shepherd metaphor was a favorite of the Lord Jesus Christ. Although the sheep/shepherd aspect refers to the church on earth, it ultimately has the invisible church in mind.

One of my favorite metaphors used to describe the nature of the church is the family of God (Luke 11:13; Romans 8:14-17; Galatians 4:5-7). The nature of the church is such that order, harmony, and unity are necessary for the church. The modern notion that families function best when the various parties are disaffected, is the very reason that churches feud, fight, and divide. If children in the family can't get along, neither can siblings in the family of God.

The Bible also describes the church as a bride (Ephesians 5:22-29). The biblical bride is supposed to be pure, and so it is with the church. The biblical bride submits to, honors, and obeys the groom. The nature of the church found in the biblical bride should show us the inseparable connection of God to his bride, the church.

Given the biblical teachings on the nature of the church, what did Jesus mean when he said, "I will build my church?" Did the Lord mean that he would build a building? Many professing Christians think of the church in terms of a physical piece of architecture. The physical structures where professing Christians meet for worship, Bible study, and fellowship have become a synonym for the church. The result is a misunderstanding of the nature of the church.

The church is God's building according to the Word of God. One verse from the Bible will make the point: "And what agreement has the temple of God with idols? For you are the temple of the living God. God has said: I will dwell in them and walk among them. I will be their God and they shall be My people" (2 Corinthians 6:16). The church in biblical terms is not a building made by men, but rather a building created in the image of God. Notice the rhetorical question asked by the inspired apostle: "What agreement has the temple of God with idols?" None of course! God is true! An idol is false! Only truth is acceptable in God's building. Falsehood and lies are unacceptable. When Christians use the term "church" in an unbiblical way, it may be a sign that they are establishing an idol.

God's building consists of the souls of Christians filled with the Holy Spirit of God. If Christians would come to grips with the nature of the church maybe the seeds of revival will germinate into beautiful plants. Many Christians do not understand the nature of the church. A generation or more grew up under a subjective set of rules that did not include a proper understanding of the fundamental principles that would have taken them down a different road.

The church in the south more than any part of the country has traditionally served as the center of social and cultural functions, thus associating the church with a building. It was the building that provided entertainment to the body rather than enrichment for the soul. The church in the Bible Belt has been treated like a social club, civic club, country club, men's club, and women's club.

Christians must set aside the baggage from previous generations. It is hard to set aside old habits, but Christians should reconsider the nature of the church and reexamine what the Bible says about the nature of the church. The church has been abused, used, and amused through the centuries. Set aside the traditional views of the church and adopt the dynamic views as you find them in the Word of God.

One substantial abuse the church has suffered since the time Thornwell wrote "The church has almost dwindled down into a secular corporation." It was true in the middle of the 19th century, but it is worse today. Many evangelicals do not understand the purpose of the church. The purpose of the church is to worship the triune God. The primary purpose of the church is to gather with other like-minded believers and offer true biblical mandated worship to God (John 4:24; Revelation 14:1-3). The church does not consist of unbelievers attending an evangelistic service.

Human beings are worshipping creatures. They are aware of their obligation to worship God whether they will admit it or not. There is a driving force built in all human beings that naturally compels them to worship so they take pleasure in worshipping as many gods as possible. It naturally follows that Christians are worshipping beings, but they must worship according to the desires and commandments of the one and only true and living God. The first four of the Ten Commandments describes who, how, and when to worship. There are many narrative descriptions of worship in the Old Testament and a less number in the New Testament. My favorite narrative text is found in the book of Jeremiah. "Thus says the Lord: 'Stand in the court of the Lord's house, and speak to all the cities of Judah, which come to worship in the Lord's house, all the words that I command you to speak to them. Do not diminish a word'" (Jeremiah 26:2). This text from Jeremiah describes a scene in the life of the Old Testament church that occurred about 2600 years ago. The one thing that the contemporary church has in common with the church of 2600 years ago is worship.

The people of God in the day of Jehoiakim the king of Judah (609-597) came to the Lord's house to worship. When the people gathered to worship, God warned the worshippers: "I will make this house like Shiloh" unless the people turn from their evil ways. The worshippers could not entertain the thought of terminating worship at Jerusalem. The worshippers were outraged and threatened to kill the preacher.

Why did they get mad at the preacher? Apparently because he said, speaking for God of course, "I (God) will make this house like Shiloh." Why was Shiloh so important? Shiloh became a place of worship for the Old Testament worshippers during the conquest under the direction of Joshua some 850 years before the scene in Jeremiah. Shiloh was the place of worship under the priesthood of Eli and his two wicked sons. After the Philistines captured the Ark of the Lord, Shiloh lost its significance and was eventually destroyed about 1050 B. C.

When Jeremiah said "this place" (the temple in Jerusalem - the place where the worshippers were presently standing) will be like Shiloh, the worshippers were real upset. The preacher was tampering with their church and their worship. Attitudes toward worship and the place believers meet for worship have not changed much in the past 2600 years. Today the murmuring might be something like "What do you mean tampering with my church! I was baptized here and I love this building or my grandfather made a considerable contribution to build this building."

Another question comes to mind. Why would God be so harsh toward those people who allegedly came to worship Him? The answer is very simple once we examine the history of worship among the Old Testament worshippers. Isaiah wrote these inspired words before the fall of the Northern Kingdom in 722 BC: "Their land has also been filled with idols; they worship the work of their hands" (Isaiah 2:8). They worship the work of their hands is equal to self-worship. John Calvin was right when he said: "men are experts at inventing idols." People love to worship man-made things. God will not tolerate self-worship. When we invent things to worship, God will depart and His judgment may be imminent. True worship has been replaced by entertainment of every sort. The application of managerial theory and psychobabble are the great enemies of true biblical worship. Today as in the day of Jeremiah, the focus is on the worshipper rather than the object of worship. It appears to me that professing Christian worshippers seem more interested in entertainment for themselves rather than worshipping the Creator. We must restore biblical worship, learn to worship God according to His pleasure and we must teach our children to worship.

True worship offered to God is either worthy worship or unworthy worship. Unworthy worship may mean the object of worship is wrong or maybe the wrong attitude toward the object of worship. Worthy worship comes from a true believer. The true object of adoration, praise and worship is the one true and living God. Worthy worship is that worship that God prescribes in His word. Worthy worship is called *theocentric* which means that *God is the center* of attention in worship. Christian worship or if you prefer the term biblical worship is directed to God, not to men, women and children. True biblical worship is not meeting someone's need. True biblical worship was not designed to necessarily minister to the needs of people, but to lift up the loving living God who does meet their needs. Since worship expresses the worthiness of God, the glory of God is the end of all true Christian worship.

If man institutes and regulates worship by the commandments of men, will God take pleasure in the worship? Contrary to popular opinion God has commanded us to worship Him according to His commandments. In an effort to appease God's wrath, false worshippers bring their man-made offerings and forms of worship to their own shame. God hates sin and He hates sinful worship.

A simple but plain fact is that all worship is not acceptable to the Lord our God. Christians cannot glorify God if they attempt to worship Him apart from His specific instructions. The Puritans called it the regulative principle of worship. The Regulative principle of worship simply means that God institutes and regulates worship according to the Word of God.

Another very unpopular, but very true biblical doctrine is that unregenerate (unsaved) human beings can only see the wrath of God. Therefore they cannot worship God the right way, even though they have a "built in" natural desire to worship. God will not accept worship from an unbeliever. Worship to the true and living God was never intended for unbelievers. In fact true worship should make unbelievers uncomfortable and maybe even outraged to the degree that they'd like to kill the preacher.

In Scripture God reveals His covenant salvation to His people as well as His covenant law so His people will know how to live. God's covenant relationship becomes real, secular and sacred through true worship.

Once Christians understand who to worship and how to worship, they will find the joy of worship is to please God.

When Christians assemble for collective worship, they are commanded not to omit, diminish, or suppress the biblical understanding of the nature and character of God. It pleases God when the church worships in spirit and truth. Christians should be filled with joy as they worship according to God's Word. Worship that is spiritual and true seeks an intimate communion with the triune God. Worshipers who worship God in Spirit and truth do so because God seeks them and they know him. They know what kind of God He is. They know and understand his sovereignty.

Evangelism, morality, education, and dozens of other good and necessary biblical disciplines have been distorted by preachers, elders, church leaders, and laymen alike to the point that theology and especially concepts like the theology of worship are despised. I witnessed this kind of distortion when a preacher of a large church said in a sermon, "The greatest deterrent to philosophy and theology…is the Word of God." Theology is a study of God. The preacher does not understand a simple principle. The Word of God is the best place to study the nature and character of God. Does the church listen to and believe the false statements made by preachers?

Worship to the true and living God is intended for believers who find joy worshipping according to God's Word so they can see their sin and trust Christ for eternal salvation. Worship is the primary purpose of the church

By now someone may ask "what about evangelism, Christian fellowship, and Christian growth?" God in His wisdom gave the church a mission and ministry so He would be glorified and His people might worship Him. The mission of the church is apostolic. The ministry includes the works of service necessary for the mission.

The Latin word *missio*, is the source for the English word mission, which refers to *a sending forth*. The Greek word *apostello*, is the source for the English word *apostle*, which refers to *one sent by authority of the sender to act on the senders behalf.* The gospels and the Acts of the Apostles' magnify the apostolic mission of the church (Matthew 28:18-20; John 17:6-18; Acts 13:1-3). The Lord Jesus Christ was sent on a mission and He sends every one of His disciples that constitute the church on a mission. The two dimensions of the mission given by injunction are to make disciples and to teach the whole counsel of God.

Evangelism is part of the process necessary to make disciples. However, instruction for the purpose of conversion is only one aspect of making disciples. Discipleship is an educational process. Christians are disciples of Christ. A disciple is simply someone who learns from a teacher. A disciple is one who learns, believes, and practices the truth. Preaching the whole counsel of God is necessary for the convert to become a disciple. Christians are students of Jesus Christ by the means appointed by God. The two primary instruments include a curriculum and a teacher. The Bible is the curriculum and ordained elders of the church are the teachers.

The Lord Jesus Christ gave the church the authority "to teach them (disciples) to observe all that I (Jesus Christ) commanded you" (Matthew 28:20). Part of the mission of the church is to teach holiness. To teach holiness means to teach the nature and character of God and to call Christians to obey the word of God in faith and practice.

Every Christian is responsible and accountable before God to participate in the mission by means of the ministry of the church. God in His wisdom gave the church a mission and ministry to accomplish the purpose of the church. The mission is to make disciples and to teach the full counsel of God. The ministry is the works of service necessary for the mission. The ministry of the church is the service of the church to those who belong to the body of Christ. Ministry is the spiritual labor of every person that belongs to the body of Christ.

The authority for ministry has been given to the church through men called to prepare God's people for works of ministry (Ephesians 4:11-16). Christ has given pastors and teachers to the church so every member in the body would be prepared to serve according to the gifts distributed by the Holy Spirit. Every Christian should be involved in the ministry of the church according to the gift that Christ gives to every individual Christian. The ministry of the church depends on the unity of the faith, full knowledge of Jesus, and spiritual maturity. A spiritually mature man in contrast to a child "tossed to and fro with every wind of doctrine" is necessary for the effective ministry of the body of Christ. The mission and ministry of the church are the instruments God has appointed to grow His church.

The church on earth cannot reach perfection, but she can anticipate perfection, in the invisible church, through the ministry of the visible church. An effective ministry means that the mission of the church (evangelism and teaching holiness) will have a foundation that will be unbreakable by every wind of doctrine and the trickery of men.

Now let's reexamine Thornwell's comment about the church. He said, "Until she becomes a spiritual body, and aims at spiritual ends by appointed means, and makes faith in God the impulsive cause of her efforts, our Zion can never arise and shine, and become a joy and a praise in the whole earth." He is right! The church will never be a joy and praise in the earth, until Christians understand the primary purpose of the church, which is worship. Thornwell says "until she becomes a spiritual body." Again he is right because the purpose of the church will be reduced to "religious clichés" if Christians do not understand the mission and ministry of the church. Therefore, the first and primary purpose of the church (worship) will be misdirected by human means rather than by spiritual appointment. The church on earth will "arise and shine, and become a joy and a praise in the whole earth" when the church uses the God appointed method for church growth.

2. Children of Modernity

Modernity has been described as "the character and system of the world produced by the forces of modernization and development."[4] "Modernization is the process that requires that our society be organized around cities for the purpose of manufacturing and commerce."[5] Modernization and Modernity are related, but different. David Wells explains modernity.

> [A] process driven by capitalism and fueled by technological innovation. These forces have reshaped our social landscape and, in turn, have reshaped our inner lives as we have been drawn into the vortex they have created. And it is this vortex that I am calling modernity.[6]

The children of modernity are the ideologies and world views that influence the public sector. Secularism, pragmatism, consumerism, relativism, individualism, and managerialism are a few of the children of modernity. The offspring that comes from these ideologies and world views produce still more offspring. The Enlightenment project gave birth to modernity and modernity has served as an agent to expand the influence of secularism. The focus of secularism as a world and life view is on the present age. If then, the attention is on the present time, why should one be concerned about anything beyond this life? The absence of this "why" question is the silent killer of evangelical Christianity. Unfortunately the focus on the secular drives Christians to become the progeny of that secular philosophy. The dilemma leads us to the sad fact that "secularized Christians rather than secular humanists...must account for the disintegration of religious vitality"[7] in the evangelical church.

The relationship between modernity and the Enlightenment project has more to do with the expression of ideas than with dogmatic philosophy. When Alasdair MacIntyre, a contemporary moral philosopher, argued that the "Enlightenment project...failed by its own standards,"[8] he went on to describe the mass of destruction it left in its path. The Enlightenment was the seed for the full development of modernity. The progeny of modernity which comes out of the Enlightenment project will be a powerful and devastating force against the evangelical church.

When liberalism threatened the church at the beginning of last century, J. Gresham Machen responded by writing an apologetic to defend the cultural mandate for Christians. Machen said, "From every point of view, therefore, the problem in question is the most serious concern of the church. What is the relation between Christianity and modern culture; may Christianity be maintained in a scientific age?"[9] Throughout the book Machen refers, at least implicitly, to the cultural mandate in the period of modernity. Christians should be ashamed for allowing culture to be controlled by the children of modernity. It is the duty of the Christian to invade the culture not for the culture to overwhelm the church. The children of modernity are the monsters invading the evangelical church.

The cultural wars in this country have their roots in theological and philosophical ideas. The cultural wars are children of modernity. James Davison Hunter argued that "The present culture war has evolved...as a struggle to establish new agreements over the character and content of America's public culture."[10] The culture wars reflect the failure of Christians to engage themselves in the God given cultural mandate. The biblical cultural mandate is "Be fruitful and multiply; fill the earth and subdue it; have dominion...over every living thing" (Genesis 1:28). While liberalism was busy changing the Christian culture through social reformation, the fundamentalists were busy building new Christian sub-cultures.

The tragedy of the effects of fundamentalism is found in the Christian sub-cultures of evangelicalism. Christian music, Christian television and radio, Christian publishing and a Christian aesthetic are just a few examples of how Christians, because of fundamentalism, have retreated from culture. On one hand they retreated from culture, but on the other they fought in the culture wars. The cultural wars are being fought over issues like education, law, politics, and ethics. The culture wars are not just dividing Christians from non-Christians; they are creating divisions among Christians. For instance, Christians are not in agreement over the abortion issue. Christians are divided over education. Culture wars were born in modernity, adopted by the fundamentalist in the church and will multiply, but to the detriment of God's people.

Another child of modernity is the therapeutic revolution. New York University professor of psychology, Dr. Paul Vitz, described America as a "psychological society in which there has been a triumph of the therapeutic."[11] Therapy has become the by-word for Americans who believe they are victims of the power and persuasion of other people. This child of modernity affects the church with its explosive appeal to the senses. God's people still have the capacity to sin and sin they do. The temptations and trials of life drive them to look for answers when they feel threatened and victimized. They go to the therapist for help and the vicious cycle continues.

Of all the children that modernity has produced, managerial madness is certainly one whose offspring will change the shape of the church. In MacIntyre's evaluation of the moral philosophy of the western world, he believed that "the bureaucratic manager...could mold, influence, and control the social environment."[12] His assessment is accurate "because sound and positive management is essential for the success of any organization"[13] according to modern managerial theory. Management has to do with the biblical concept of stewardship. Management is not a new concept, but modernity has exploited it and made it a tool, which works against the biblical concept of stewardship.

The progeny of modernity will continue to influence the evangelical church, unless the church learns how to control the monstrous children of modernity. These children of modernity are not intrinsically evil, but they may become instruments of the enemy to bring about evil. Evangelical Christians should understand the dangers of these children. Os Guinness quotes Peter Berger to caution the church about using the children of modernity. "He warns that whoever sups with the devil of modernity had better have a long spoon."[14] More must be said about this warning.

> The believer who sups with it will find his spoon getting shorter and shorter – until that last supper in which he is left alone at the table, with no spoon at all and with an empty plate. Our challenge, then, is to dine at the banquet of modernity – but with long spoons.[15]

With this good warning the evangelical church should be appraised of the dangers, but make use of the benefits of modernity.

As an unbeliever I always thought I had more authority than power. As a Christian I realize I have more power than authority. I have the power to sin, but not the authority. I have the power to be theologically wrong, but I do not have the authority to be theologically wrong. There is a sense of power flowing forth from the children of modernity. David Wells argues that "what shapes the modern world is not powerful minds but powerful forces, not philosophy but urbanization, capitalism and technology."[16] He is correct and brings attention to the inevitable relationship between the modern and the postmodern.

The postmodern mind is not necessarily empty, but it is not stimulated by an intellectual agenda. In postmodernism the scholar has replaced the intellectual. The modern scholar schooled by a teacher does not apply the rules of logic into intellectual inquiry. Every aspect of life is reinterpreted by the postmodern so that tradition will not enter the scene. The postmodern world rejects objective rationality in favor of a critical legal theory, education theory, et al. The postmodern hermeneutic has affected evangelicalism in the area of grammatical/historical interpretation more than any other dimension of the postmodern world. The postmodern interpretation requires the deconstruction of the text. It may be said that "postmodernist theories begin with the assumption that language cannot render truths about the world in an objective way."[17] Deconstructionism may be the majority report in the future of literary analysis, but that does not necessarily make it the right choice. Another voice explaining postmodern thought said "The one thing I have learned in hermeneutics which has changed everything is what I can only call 'obedience to the text' – listening to the text itself instead of modern interpreters of it."[18] The postmodern deconstructionist can make no claim for truth because truth cannot be defined except for deconstructing the text. Thomas Oden corrects this error using the intellectual powers to define absolutes. To understand the non-structure and powerlessness of postmodernism will help one understand the structure and power of modernity.

The power of modernity is rooted in the relativism that springs from it. "It is a period whose key general features (moral relativism, narcissism hedonism, naturalistic reductionism, and autonomous individualism) have been well described by modern intellectual historians... ."[19] Relativism as a philosophy has stood in front of every part of our society including religion and philosophy. Relativism is powerful, because it cannot be contained in any body of thought. The children of modernity are poised to use relativism to advance their cause and it is a powerful tool. Relativism is inherently dangerous in modern thought.

> Relativization has its own special hazards, and important distinctions must be preserved. Historicism's rejection of transcendence subjects its followers to the same dizzying loss of stability that Einsteinian physics created for categories of time and space... .Everything is relativized because there is nothing transcending the flux that could provide the stability needed to position everything else... .The kind of relativization that can be affirmed, in contrast, is that which places human values under the judgment of the transcendent God... .A society that cannot tolerate a judge beyond history will find that it can learn to tolerate anything else.[20]

The "judge beyond history" has a fixed unchangeable standard for His created order. If Christians reject His

standard, then they have the awful face of relativism which
will lead to compromise and confusion.

Without sounding redundant let me emphasize that I make
a distinction between scholars and intellectuals. A scholar is
one who has been trained and practices a particular school of
thought. For instance, there are many scholars loaded with
volumes of propaganda and who are well equipped to
champion a cause. I ask you to consider the politically correct
crowd. They are well schooled, but their arguments break
down on the debate table. Intellectuals on the other hand
wrestle with the world of ideas. They pursue lines of thought
using logical processes that come to definite conclusions.
Therefore, scholars are subject to relativization, but
intellectuals are bound to analytical and logical processes
leading to an absolute.

The impact of relativization on the evangelical church
reflects the power of modernity. How certain it is that "many
are of the mind that [the] Christian faith is only relatively
true... ."[21] The disappearance of absolute truth in the Christian
arena is a devastating blow to the mission of the church. A
right view of the mission of the church will be evident when
the church once again embraces absolute truth.

The Children of Modernity may cause Christians to
struggle with their identity. Christians do not have to struggle
for identity. The essential characteristics of Christians, truly
professing and practicing Christians, are outlined in the
beatitudes (Matthew 5:3-11). The Sermon on the Mount, as it
is commonly called, is for God's children. Jesus gives a

definition of a Christian in the Sermon on the Mount. The Sermon on the Mount is often approached from the ethical dimension. For just a moment, I want to consider the indicative dimension of the Beatitudes because they refer to the essence of Christianity rather than the practice of Christianity.

When Jesus announced the "blessings" in Matthew chapter five, He ended them by saying "Blessed are those who have been persecuted for the sake of righteousness..." Persecution comes because natural man hates God. "The wrath of God is being revealed from heaven against all the godlessness and wickedness of men who suppress the truth by their wickedness" (Romans 1:18). Jonathan Edwards said "man is naturally totally ignorant of God in His divine Excellency." Edwards is not saying that natural man is totally ignorant of God, but totally ignorant of the majesty of the divine Excellency of God. Every human has some knowledge of God. Those who have not been born again by the spirit of God hate what they know about God. Those who have been spiritually re-born by the Spirit of God have a saving knowledge of God's sweetness and Excellency. The Christian is then blessed according to the eight benedictions given by Jesus in the Beatitudes.

A person who has been blessed should become a blessing to others. If you are a Christian, you're like salt and light. Jesus describes what Christians are like in response to a society that hates God and seeks to persecute God's servants. Jesus uses a metaphor to describe the Christian state of being referred to as "like salt and light." If you are like salt and light, then your actions will reflect your state of being. A horse acts like a horse, because a horse is a horse. It is a simple statement, but it is loaded with philosophical and theological profundity. It sounds so simple, let's try another statement. A Christian acts like a Christian because a Christian is a Christian. Jesus explains why in the Gospel of Matthew. Jesus uses two metaphors, salt and light, to describe a Christian.

Jesus said "you are the salt of the earth." We know this is not a literal statement, because a Christian is more than a chemical composition known as sodium chloride. Salt is used in Scripture in a literal sense to flavor and season food, to preserve and cleanse, and to render useless. It is also used as a figure of speech. Jesus uses "salt" as a figure in this text to describe those Christians who act as a preservative in society. Salt not only preserves, it nourishes. Christians serve as a means of spiritual nourishment to a deprived and depraved society. Salt also symbolically serves as an agent to make land unproductive. Christians will make the works of Satan unproductive by teaching and preaching the truth while they pray for reformation. Finally, salt creates thirst. Are you a salty Christian? Do you stand for truth? Most Christians say they believe the truth, but can they defend the truth? Statistics indicate there are approximately 94 million evangelical Christians in the United States. If that is true, why is America rapidly becoming one of the most pagan (un-Christian) nations in the western world?

Jesus said, "you are the light of the world." He goes on to say you are the light if you "let your light shine before men, that they may see your good deeds..." Natural man is in spiritual darkness, but the person who is born again by the Spirit of God is walking in the light and it must show. Jesus puts it in the form of a command, "Let your light shine before men." Do you hide your righteousness from the unconverted person who desires to persecute you? Do you hide your righteousness from the converted person who might mock your Christian walk? Consider! Children of God should say like the Psalmist, "My heart shall rejoice in Thy salvation" (Psalm 13:5). One way to experience the joy of salvation is to be salt and light in an unsavory and dark world.

Christians are blessed because they do not have to struggle for identity. Their identity is in their source of being, the Lord Jesus Christ. By the grace of God, the love of Christ, and the power of the Holy Spirit, Christians will rejoice that they know who they are and how to live.

3. The Influence of Modernity

Modernity offers variety and change to any who will make their vows to it. The secret to the success of modernity's expansion is rationalism. The sense in which I am referring to rationalism is the appeal to reason, apart from sense experience. Modernity's rationalism is the only way to solve problems and ultimately to find salvation. There is a distinction between a rationalist, one who uses reason in an attempt to interpret reality and rationalism as I have just described. Rationalism does not answer all the questions of life and reality. The Bible has the answers to reality and life.

> Jacques Barzun has pointed out that eighteenth century Liberalism (the cult of self) and eighteenth century Rationalism (the cult of reason) had the effect of making religion seem superfluous. If man is his own master, and reason his only judge, what is man to do with the lingering sense that there is more to life than his reason and the material world can contain?[22]

Rationalism ends up in the world of subjectivity. The quest to understand reality never completes the cycle, so the next step is to try something new or different. The students of modernity have mastered this concept. It is sad but true that the evangelical church has been persuaded by these disciples to become the vehicle to spread the message of modernity.

Modernity has powerful persuasive elements, which indicate that "Modernity is not just a time but a set of passions, hopes, and ideas, a mentality that prevails in some circles more than in others, and nowhere more than the university, the primary agent of the ideology of modernity."[23] The university is the place our theologians go for an education. Many seminaries have university trained professors. The unanswered question is searching. To what extent have professing Christian preachers, teachers, and theologians been persuaded by modernity and how much of that persuasion will be passed on to the coming generations? The evangelical church stands on the edge of the precipice of a plunge into a neo dark age. Should we be fearful that modernity is standing ready to push the church over the edge?

The potential threat of modernity to the evangelical church is probably greater than ever, but the opportunity for reformation is also greater than any time in recent history. The children of modernity have attempted to secularize Christianity. We see this a number of different ways, but primarily as "the pastor seeks to embody what modernity admires and to redefine what pastoral ministry now means in light of this culture's two most admired types, the manager and the psychologist."[24] David Wells attributes the problem to the disappearance of theology. If sound theology disappears then something must replace that theology. I ask you to consider "The gulf between the truth-centered evangelism of Edwards and Whitefield and the technique-centered variety of industrialized religion...illustrated by Charles Finney... ."[25]

Finney's method of evangelism is one of many examples of how modernity threatens the good health of the evangelical church. Although Finney's theology is not well systematized, it is well documented that he believed *methods* were the key to the salvation of a soul. Likewise, the church growth movement believes that methods will fill the pews.

Modernity has produced a progeny by its power and persuasion and now poses a threat to the church. What can we do? We can reject the "myths of power [and] popularity, [which] have led to an unhealthy preoccupation with superficial success, methods over message, technique over truth, quantity over quality"[26] The greater question is how can we accomplish this? Mike Horton responds to the question by reminding us of our world and life view.

> The Bible commands, "Do not conform any longer to the pattern of this world, but be transformed by the renewing of your mind" (Romans 12:2). While much fuel has been spent on trying to get people to act like Christians, the Bible insists that we must first think like Christians. The transforming of our minds takes place not through magic, superstitious techniques, or superficial devotions, but through serious and sometimes difficult study. It requires that we know something about the Bible and the people to whom it is addressed, and that we know something about ourselves and the culture in which we live. It is dangerous to pretend one is not worldly when one

refuses to critically examine the ways in which one has been influenced more by the spirit of the age than by the Spirit of Christ.[27]

The Christian world and life view does not spring forth from the ground like an artesian well. It is formulated by the laborious effort of the individual empowered by the Holy Spirit. Christians do not devote enough time and effort asking the *why* questions of the Christian faith. Why should the church use the tools of modernity is the question Christians must ask? But all too often Christians ask, "how may I use the tools of modernity?" rather than running from them. Christians often ask the scientific question *how* rather than the philosophical question *why*. The *why* question will always need to consult the Word of God to find the correct answer. The Christian begins to use the tools of modernity, relativism creeps in and soon methodology becomes their god. "In 1926 the Bible Crusaders of America formed: its special mission was to combat Modernism, Evolution, Agnosticism and Atheism."[28] Today evangelicals are no longer contending against Modernism, they are embracing it. The most notable example of this can be found in the church growth movement.

4. Goals of the Church Growth Movement

The church growth movement is a loose confederation of ministers and laymen whose beginning can be traced to Donald McGavran. He was a missionary to India, professor at Fuller Seminary and founder of the Church Growth Institute.

The church growth movement does not have the privilege of pointing to any significant theologian in their ranks. When Martin Luther and John Calvin stood in the gap during the early years of the Reformation, it would not be improper to refer to them as part of a movement that sought to be reformed by the Word of God. Although some of the key men in the Reformation had points of disagreement, they were bound together by a common theology. The church growth movement is void of any theological center. The movement may be found in liberal, conservative, fundamental, or evangelical churches. It may be said that proponents of the church growth movement are bound together by a common philosophy. What is the glue that keeps them together?

Leaders of the church growth movement surround themselves with disciples that have the appearance of a personality cult. Win Arn, a noted disciple of Donald McGavran, said, "trainees who come out of victorious churches and have been trained by men, who are themselves multipliers of churches, are generally effective."[29] The idea is that success breeds success. It has been suggested that the concept of a *flagship church* should be used as a model.

It must be emphasized that the term 'Flagship Church'
is a functional definition. Just as the simplest definition
of a leader is 'a person people follow,' so a flagship
church is a functional designation of a church which
has a fruitful, pace setting ministry within a given
metropolitan area.[30]

This leadership concept seems to be the norm among
church growth movement teachers, yet some of them look to
Scripture to defend their leadership concept. In one case,
Nehemiah and Paul were used as the examples cited by
adherents of the church growth movement. The *Handbook for
Church Growth* described John Calvin as "a man of great
organizational and leadership ability."[31]

Yes, these men are examples of great leaders, but they did
not try to gather other church leaders into a "follow me" plan.
These men attempted and had some success in reforming the
church, according to the Word of God. The popular concept
among the church growth movement leaders is a "follow the
successful leader" plan. One leader in the church growth
movement "sponsors a conference [three times a year] at
which 500 church leaders gather to see how it is done."[32]

The best guide to know how God wants to grow His
church is the Bible. The biblical concept for expanding the
kingdom of God is: one plants, one waters, and one reaps the
harvest, but God alone causes the church to grow. A
fundamental error in the church growth movement is when

pastors are told they can expect their churches to grow, but "they must be willing to follow a growth leader."[33]

The pastor is expected to assume the Chief Executive Officer position. George Barna, a leader in church growth methodology, boldly critiques the church by saying, "many people do judge the pastor not on his ability to preach, teach, or counsel, but on his capacity to make the church run smoothly and efficiently. In essence he is judged as a businessman..."[34] The evidence is compelling. The church growth movement is an alliance of professing Christian leaders who are committed to the same goal. What is that goal?

Church Growth is the goal! Church growth movement advocates define church growth as "that science which investigates the planting, multiplication, function, and health of Christian churches as they relate specifically to the effective implementation of God's commission... ."[35] Another church growth movement guru stated their philosophy a different way.

> One of the basic premises of the church growth movement is that efforts in evangelism can be measured and that the effectiveness of methods can be evaluated and the responses of people and fields can also be gauged. Perhaps the most basic premise is that God intends for his church to grow and the church growth must be pursued out of obedience to Jesus Christ.[36]

The scientific method is useful for measuring, evaluating, and bringing theories to a conclusion. It is not useful if it impinges upon mandates given in Scripture. I cannot find a hint in Scripture for the church to measure the effectiveness of God's evangelistic method. What is clear in Scripture is the mandate for Christians to be involved in the evangelistic enterprise. The problem with the church growth movement is not its desire to be involved in evangelism, but rather the method used in evangelism. Methodology is the culprit. The method used by the church growth movement resembles a multi-level marketing scheme. A dynamic, charismatic and persuasive leader looks for other people who are dynamic, charismatic, and persuasive. With these personalities, add transferable concepts and then church growth will follow. Donald McGavran uses different words to say the same thing: "That sort of training of leaders marked Pastor Kennedy's work at Coral Ridge. He took people one by one and trained them to present the gospel effectively. The results in his church have been outstanding."[37] It all sounds good, but is that the biblical way? Is their methodology biblical?

They would argue that church growth is biblical. Since church growth is de facto biblical, they set out to offer Scripture proofs. The fallacy is that no Christian can deny that church growth is not biblical. Robertson McQuilkin, former President of Columbia Bible College and Seminary, wrote a paper, "How Biblical Is The Church Growth Movement," that was later published in book form. The book entitled *Measuring the Church Growth Movement* was first published in 1973. He argued strongly that the church growth movement followed biblical principles. Mr. McQuilkin posits, "the underlying presuppositions of the Church Growth Movement rest on solid theological foundations grounded in the Word of God."[38] He went on to say, "the principle that the church is God's means for accomplishing His purposes in world evangelization is one such obvious principle."[39] The problem with that statement is the interpretation of words. What does the word *church* mean to Mr. McQuilkin? I will make some assertions based on my experience while I was a student at Columbia Bible College, which may help us interpret these quotes from his book. While he was President of Columbia Bible College and Seminary he actively promoted para-church ministries with a passionate devotion. His passion for para-church ministries diluted the work of the church. It is said that "para-church organizations" work alongside the church. There is no biblical merit to that statement. Mr. McQuilkin was rather bold about his view of the church. He said, "in the evangelistic responsibility of the church, Pacific Broadcasting Association may have special responsibility for proclamation, [and] Billy Graham may have special responsibility for persuasion... ."[40] The Pacific Broadcasting Association is not the church. Furthermore, Billy Graham who is a fine man in many regards had assumed a leadership position, but not in the church. The Billy Graham Evangelistic Association is a para-church ministry. As an outspoken Arminian Mr. McQuilkin's church growth strategy is also Arminian. Arminian doctrine relative to salvation and evangelism depends on man's work

and ability rather than God's sovereignty. In his book, Mr.
McQuilkin makes an explicit statement to that effect.

> I mean proclaiming the way to life in Christ in such a
> way as to give men a clear understanding of this good
> news so that they may choose to become His disciples
> and a part of His church...I mean persuading men,
> reconciling to God those men who have been alienated
> from Him... ."[41]

C. Peter Wagner agrees with Mr. McQuilkin. Wagner
believes that "the goal of evangelism is to persuade men and
women to become disciples of Jesus Christ and to serve him in
the fellowship of his church."[42] The ability of man is the
emphasis rather than the sovereignty of God and these are not
isolated examples. There have been others in the church
growth movement who used "The Four Spiritual Laws"[43] as
an evangelistic method. The church growth movement and
Arminian doctrine agree that human ability is the means for
salvation and church growth.

The goal of the church growth movement is church growth
and that is accomplished by means of evangelism. However,
they seem to forget that evangelism is only one of several
duties God requires of Christians. Evangelism is the top
priority on their agenda. They almost dismiss the fundamental
purpose of the church, which is to worship the triune God.
Evangelism is not the purpose of the church; it is part of the
mission of the church. They also forget the need for a common
confession. "Like the deists in 1776, evangelicals today are

suspicious of creeds, confessions, and doctrinal systems."[44] This charge by Horton seems to be very much at home in the church growth movement. They have no common theological system and no common doctrinal statement, just a basic common philosophy based on the common goal for church growth.

5. Philosophy of the Church Growth Movement

The basic philosophy of the church growth movement is to use the children of modernity to cause the church to grow. Even so followers still struggle with the church growth movement philosophy.

> J. Randall Petersen...is involved in starting Hope United Methodist Church...To gather its congregation, Hope Church used a telemarketing campaign to invite community members to its services...He is still uneasy with some church-growth ideas...But it worked, he admits...Petersen is not alone in his pragmatic embrace of church-growth thinking.[45]

Pragmatism is one of the basic philosophies of the church growth movement. "'If it works, use it' captures the spirit of pragmatism."[46] This is demonstrated by the intense effort to meet the "felt needs" of professing Christians. A felt need is described as "the conscious wants and desires of a person."[47] The pragmatic view attempts to see that "sermons are short, simple, uplifting and personally inspiring. Topics are carefully selected to stress the personal over the doctrinal and the relational over the abstract."[48] "Christianity Today" reports that during the growing days of the movement "church growth was soon marked by strong pragmatism."[49] When I discuss biblical evangelism with Christians who use Arminian methods, most of the time they will defend their method by saying, "but it works." Is it conceivable that Christians believe that pragmatism is the criteria by which we engage in God's kingdom work? Pragmatism has replaced Scripture as the final authority to direct how we may serve God. Pragmatism takes many forms in the church growth movement. One is the idea that target groups will achieve church growth. It has been said that "The PCA has church planting efforts not only in establishing Anglo churches but also ethnic churches among Koreans, Japanese, Hispanics, and Blacks in the United States."[50] But, I ask you how many Black churches have they started, or even attempted to start in Jackson, Mississippi or Montgomery, Alabama? The multi-ethnic philosophy sounds good, but it would not be pragmatic to try it in cities such as I have just mentioned. There is some merit to the homogeneous-unit principle, "but practically, church marketers exclusively target white, middle-class, college educated baby boomers, born between 1946 and 1964. Other groups are rarely mentioned."[51]

The pragmatic strategy of the church growth movement demands an embrace of the managerial system of modernity. A lengthy quote is necessary to explain how this works.

> Defining goals and objectives, and making them understandable to each member of the church is the most important leadership task before us. It is difficult and it takes discipline. Robert Townsend in *Up The*

Organization describes the lengthy and difficult process at Avis in setting objectives. 'One of the important functions of a leader is to make the organization concentrate on it objectives. In the case of Avis, it took us six months to define one objective – which turned out to be: We want to become the fastest growing company with the highest profit margin in the business of renting and leasing vehicles without drivers.[52]

The goal of Avis Rent a Car and the church are entirely different. Avis has one purpose and that is to make money to pay the investors and remain in business. The purpose of the church is to glorify the Lord God Almighty, not accumulate the almighty dollar. Then why do these church leaders try to draw an analogy between Avis and the church? The Bible teaches us to be good stewards of all that God has given to us, but our theology must dictate the methods of stewardship. Is it improper to advertise or even use telemarketing? There is nothing wrong with these tools, unless they become gods. Inviting people to worship may not be the right thing to do, because if they are unconverted they are not able to worship God. The unconverted need to be evangelized and then invited to worship. Inviting someone to come to church is a non-sensible idea. As I said before no one can "come to church." The church goes to worship, Bible study, fellowship, etc.

Pragmatism does not understand the law of God, or the grace of God. The law and the gospel are on the endangered species list, because of the awful abuse in recent years. Martin Luther said, "the difference between the Law and the Gospel is the height of knowledge in Christendom."[53] The reformers did not attempt to replace the law and the gospel with anything, because everything in the Bible came under the law or the gospel. "We divide this Word into two principal parts or kinds: the one is called the 'Law,' the other the 'Gospel.' All the rest can be gathered under the one or the other of these two headings."[54] Pragmatism may accomplish what is perceived as church growth, but the people may be deceived when something else replaces the preaching of the law of God. Without the law of God how can anyone understand God's love? God's law cannot be ignored. Just because pragmatism causes a church to grow does not give pragmatism approval in the sight of God.

> According to the pragmatic interpretation of evangelical faith, Christianity has to compete with other self-help programs. It has to promise health, wealth, and happiness. But what happens when something works better.[55]

The church must have a standard so objective goals for church growth meet with reality. If the church will follow the regulative principle found in the Word of God then there is no possibility of finding something better.

The pragmatic agenda works as well for the Jehovah's Witness or Mormons as it does for the evangelical church. For example, the church growth movement theorists use an assessment center to determine whether or not a man (and his wife?) has the qualifications and potential to start a new church. The fundamental theory behind the assessment center would work just as well for the Church of the Latter Day Saints as it would for a Presbyterian Church. That is the reason liberals and conservatives alike may attend the assessment center. The assessment center is a pragmatic utilitarian psychologically man-made program. Church growth movement advocates argue for this method of selecting men to plant new churches because they say it works better than the old programs! Of course, a man-centered assessment will result in a man-centered ministry.

The story of the man of God from Judah in 1 Kings 13 is a good example of how God deals with ungodly pragmatism. The man of God was instructed by God to go to a particular place, execute a particular task, and return home without eating bread or drinking water. A prophet seduced the man of God to eat and drink, which he did, but God punished him for his disobedience. No doubt, it was a matter of prudence and pragmatism to be refreshed before completing the trip, but God had spoken. God's covenant structure is not compromising or pragmatic. There are blessings for those who keep the covenant and cursed is the man who breaks the covenant.

Dr. Guinness is right. If we dine with pragmatism, we should "have a long spoon." The temptations of modernity are tremendous. Pragmatic utility is not necessarily sinful, but pragmatism may become sinful if accepted uncritically. The church growth movement has adopted the god of pragmatism by its "uncritical use of such insights and tools of modernity as management and marketing."[56] The church will come under the judgment of God if she uses a poll to determine the truth. "For the sake of 'seeker sensitivity,' preaching remains superficial, with thousands of confessing Christians fed a weekly diet of entry-level evangelism."[57]

Another basic philosophy of the church growth movement that comes from the modern table is consumerism. This world and life view is not an illusion, although it is connected with the use of modern imagery. Consumerism has been molded by the cast of modernity. The church growth movement has deified consumerism rather than treating it as an omen of modernity. A consumer is one who uses a commodity or service. The consumer integrates pragmatism and utilitarianism to produce consumerism. Christians, especially in this present time, are consumers, but God is not a product. To put that in evangelical terms: "We are not selling a product to a consumer, but proclaiming a Savior to a sinner."[58]

The church growth movement teaches that marketing the church is necessary for church growth. Consider the progression in the following sentences from the church growth movement treatment of the subject:

'The Church is a business.'/'Marketing is essential for a business to operate successfully.'/'The Bible is one of the world's great marketing texts.'/'However, the point is indisputable: the Bible does not warn against the evils of marketing.'/'So it behooves us not to spend time bickering about techniques and processes.'/'Think of your church not as a religious meeting place, but as a service agency – an entity that exists to satisfy people's needs... .[59]

The syllogism sounds reasonable, except "meeting needs" does not always satisfy needs; it often stokes further needs and raises the pressure of eventual disillusionment. As Immanuel Kant said to the Russian historian Karamzin, "Give a man everything he desires and yet at this very moment he will feel that everything is not everything." The outcome is a massive pandering to the pathology of a consumerist age."[60] The gods created by man will never satisfy the deepest yearning of the soul. Across the pages of history hedonism and narcissism were more than world and life views, they became gods in the eyes of unbelievers and professing Christians. Even in the church, Tetzel sold indulgences much like television preachers sell the gospel in our time. Likewise, the church growth movement has knuckled under to the pressure from modernity.

The fundamental goal, however sad, but true, is that most Christians want to be happy from a secular perspective. All of life is shaped around the desire to be self-fulfilled and happy. The French Revolution certainly had a profound influence on the concept of happiness. Liberty, equality, and fraternity redefined happiness for every successive generation. The worldview we call   consumerism suggests that happiness comes from instant gratification.

Selling Jesus is an art for the church growth experts. Evangelism is no longer God-centered, but rather it is consumer-centered. Christian singers try to dazzle the audience with sensational music. Preachers preach to *felt needs* using popular aphorisms, rarely expounding from the inerrant Word of God or using sound exegetical and hermeneutical skills.

The strategy for marketing the church may very well be a death angel in disguise. A pastor responded to an article written in "Christianity Today" on June 24, 1991 about the church growth movement.

> My concern with the movement is that it prompts the question, 'What is the difference between the Christian church and any other business that makes use of telemarketing, demographic, and other mainstream corporate resources?' Are we saying the church is a business just like any other business – only our message is different? If this is so, possibly pastoral training should lean heavier in the direction of marketing, business, and advertising skills and less on theology, biblical scholarship, and pastoral counseling classes.[61]

Obviously the writer of that article, Rev. David Coffin, is not an advocate of the church growth movement and apparently he is aware that many seminaries have moved toward teaching church marketing rather than theology. Seminaries are responding to the *felt needs* of theological students. But, that is what they want. "Yesterday McDonalds sold only hamburgers and fish; today you can eat breakfast there! In their vocations, our people [church leaders at Bear Valley Baptist Church, Denver, Colo.] have been taught to think, how can we improve, expand our markets, do a better job?"[62] Implied here is the idea that like McDonalds, the church must find out what people want and what makes them happy and provide it without considering the theological implications. The church growth movement has compromised and capitulated essential theological standards to the point that their disciples have turned their backs from the marks of the church.

Christians ought to investigate the variety of world views found in the modern world. The Christian world view is fundamentally rooted in the supernaturalism of the triune God. The Christian world view, as previously mentioned, is characterized by a philosophy of absolute truth. What is truth? Theologians and philosophers in all ages wrestle with this question. It is said that truth is that which is in agreement to that which is represented and truth corresponds to reality, so you might say that truth is that which conforms to fact or reality. Christians have the Bible to help them understand the truth relative to the excellencies of God and the sinfulness of man. Jesus manifestly explained how unbelievers do not understand biblical truth (John 8:43-47). The Bible is truth.

"The sum of Thy word is truth" (Psalm 119:160) and
Christians must be affected by the truth. "Thou are near, O
Lord, and all Thy commandments are truth" (Psalm 119:151).
Moral truth will affect every part of the Christian life. Moral
truth is rooted in the integrity of God therefore truth is an
attribute of God, which God has chosen to share with His
church. The Bible teaches that there is saving power in truth.
"But as for me, my prayer is to Thee, O Lord, at an acceptable
time; O God, in the greatness of Thy lovingkindness answer
me with Thy saving truth" (Psalm 69:13). It is the duty of all
Christians to think about God's truth. The Bible tells us to
take "every thought captive to the obedience of Christ" (2
Corinthians. 10:5). Today Christians are being lulled to sleep
and Satan's deceptive tricks try to convince Christians that
truth is relative and there is no difference between truth and
error. However we live in a postmodern world that declares all
objective real truth is dead. Modernity believes that truth is
discoverable though investigation based on worldviews that
allegedly lead to ultimate truth. If modernity is the god of the
church growth movement, how does the movement discover
truth? This question remains to be answered because the
church growth movement has no theological center upon
which to determine truth.

6. Church Growth Movement Pulpits

The Reformers identified the "preaching of the Word of God"[63] as one of the true marks of the church. The church growth movement adherents may acknowledge the marks of the church during licensure and ordination examinations, but they fail to practice them with any consistency.

Ministers advocating the church growth movement would say that they preach a sermon, but not traditional style. Then the difficulty of determining what constitutes the "preaching of a sermon" must be determined. First, we must look at the biblical examples. There are some excellent sermons in most of the Old Testament prophetical books. Then Jesus and the Apostles have a number of sermons that may be analyzed. Throughout the history of the church there are voluminous sermons recorded so we may determine the nature and character of the "preaching of a sermon."

Preaching a sermon includes the whole counsel of God. It includes sin, hell, judgment and holiness on one hand and grace, forgiveness, and heaven on the other hand. My research included the examination of books related directly to the church growth movement relative to the discipline of preaching. Unfortunately, little was said about preaching the whole counsel of God. It is true that preaching has been the subject of scorn among churchmen throughout the ages. Early last century J. Gresham Machen warned the evangelical church "the absence of doctrinal teaching and preaching...in the church"[64] would have a bad effect. Preaching has been described as the "careful exposition of the Scriptures with relevant and close application of it in boldness tempered with humility.[65] The nineteenth century Southern Presbyterian theologian, Dr. Robert L. Dabney, has said that "The preacher's task may be correctly explained as that of (instrumentally) forming the image of Christ upon the souls of men."[66] The sermons of Luther, Calvin, Edwards, and Whitefield are all examples of God-centered preaching compared to the pep talks coming from the pulpits of the church growth movement.

> Messages are purposefully kept light and simple, humorous and anecdotal, in order to keep the audience. The audience never becomes a congregation. The weekly sermon designed for unchurched Harry never makes the transition from performance to proclamation. Harry may feel better, but he remains spiritually unchanged.[67]

The preaching and teaching ministry of the church is one of the primary means to accomplish the mission and ministry of the church. The prophet Ezekiel was commissioned by God as a watchman (Ezekiel 33:1-11). In the Old Testament a watchman may serve in one of several capacities. Watchmen were stationed on city walls so they could alert the city if hostile action threatened the city. Watchmen were also appointed to watch over fields and vineyards during the time of harvest. The Bible uses the term watchman as an allegorical device to describe a prophet as a watchman for God. It was the duty of the watchman to announce to the people of God either good news or impending doom as the case may be. Interestingly enough Ezekiel had already been taken captive to Babylon and apparently ministered to a group of Jewish captives by the River Chebar. You might call them the underground church of the Old Testament.

Ezekiel spoke words of hope concerning the restoration of the Old Testament saints to the land of their forefathers. Ezekiel also spoke words of judgment to the Old Testament saints in exile. His warning was: turn now to the Lord, because God delighted in those who turned from sin. Ezekiel's words are as fresh as this morning's newspaper and we need to hear afresh the Word of God delivered from the mouthpiece of God. The mouthpiece of God must announce to the people of God the law and the gospel for the benefit of their own spiritual nurture and growth.

The evangelical church is at a point of crisis. All too often the shepherds are slumbering and not watching for the wolves as they subtly come into and separate the flock. The apostle Paul said by inspiration from God "if any man is preaching to you a gospel contrary to that which you received, let him be accursed" (Galatians 1:9). He also said "Some to be sure, are preaching Christ even from envy and strife, but some also from good will" (Philippians 1:15).

Too much preaching today is contrary to biblical preaching. Preaching the Word of God has a fragrance. To some it smells bad and to others it smells good. Some preaching smells good to God and some smells bad.

7. Church Growth Becomes a Movement

The church growth movement is a movement, but to further clarify it is an unbiblical movement. The church militant has contended with movements throughout its history. The church growth movement is not much different than many others founded on human philosophy. Its founder, Donald McGavran, taught at a liberal seminary, was in a liberal denomination (The Disciples of Christ) and it is not feasible to think that his world and life view, theology, and doctrine was not affected by those people who surrounded him. McGavran and his movement are the products of modernity. His disciples have followed in his steps and they drink deeply from the streams of modernity. They are not committed to classical Christianity but instead "the religious leadership withheld its gift and whored after each successive stage of modernity's profligacy."[68] The danger of the church growth movement is found in its god – modernity. They have made no attempt to identify their theology or doctrine. In fact, they have "attempted not to allow church growth teaching to identify itself with any particular paradigm of systematic theology. Church growth principles have intentionally been kept as atheological as possible... ."[69] Michael Horton pointed out the danger by reminding the church that "a rejection of theology is a rejection of Scripture, inasmuch as the Bible is filled with propositional statements about the character of God."[70]

Church growth movement advocates do not seem to understand the concept of church growth. If the methodology of the movement is brought under critical analysis using biblical standards, the reply goes something like this: "When church growth is attacked today, it is usually done by persons who, not having had the opportunity to think their way through the morass, are comforting themselves with the old rationalizations of defeat."[71] It is not church growth that suffers this critique, it is the church growth movement's affinity to the *god* of the movement, which is *modernity* rather than the *God* of the *Bible*.

An evaluation of the church growth movement will reveal the preponderance of modernity in their scheme. The "church growth movement is a matter of both ideas that serve ideals and ideas that serve interests."[72] If the ideals and interests were on behalf of the true and living God, then the church growth movement would be a blessing. However, the weight of the evidence is that the church growth movement has self-serving ideals and interests.

The church growth movement is carrying the banner of modernity and there is no indication that the church growth movement will inquire of the dangers of modernity and turn from them. There is an antithesis to be considered:

> The Christian mind has sought and found a way to understand life in the light of revelation; the modern mind rejects that light and turns instead to private experience for illumination. The Christian mind

accepts God's pronouncements concerning the meaning of life as the only true measure in that regard; the modern mind rejects such revelation as the figment of a religious imagination.[73]

The more room Christians give modernity, the less room they give the true and living God. The church growth movement openly admits to embrace the children of modernity, but remove themselves from sound biblical doctrine and theology. Our Lord teaches, "No one can serve two masters; for either he will hate the one and love the other, or he will hold to one and despise the other. You cannot serve God and mammon."[74]

The church growth movement could make a contribution to the health of the church if they will turn from modernity's control and define their nature and purpose biblically and theologically. "Without any authorized definition of a movement's teaching, it cannot span the generations or even assess the validity of potential misinterpretations."[75] We will do well to remember the tensions we face with the concept of church growth.

The sense of helplessness that prevails among our people...is a serious indictment of the crisis in which we find ourselves. Therefore when we speak of the need of the reflective growth of the church, we are speaking of something of critical importance, affecting the future of the cosmos.[76]

One of the greatest minds of the western world in modern times was Jonathan Edwards and even he struggled with the pressing forces of modernity. I hope the God of biblical church growth will direct the church growth movement so that the adherents of that movement might enjoy our Father in heaven.

Although the adoption of a pantheon of gods by the church growth movement is obvious, the most obvious god of the church growth movement is modernity. The compelling evidence is that the church growth movement finds satisfaction with those false gods rather than with the one true and living God.

The growth of other unbiblical movements such as the Promise Keepers added fuel to the fire for the church growth movement. The Promise Keepers was organized by a former football coach and promoted by men who think they are above the authority of church. Bill Bright and James Dobson are examples of men who promote their agendas and the Promise Keepers agenda through Para-church organizations rather than coming under the authority and ministry of the church.

The growth and success of the church growth movement may be attributed to ill equipped and patronizing ministers. They are more interested in their own private agendas than in the clear teaching of the Word of God.

The hope for the future of the church is not in the church growth movement, but in the powerful work of God through the hands of faithful churchmen who are being reformed by the Word of God.

Appendix A

Originally published in the theological newsletter, *Informed and Reformed*, February 1996

An assessment of Assessment Centers used by advocates of the church growth movement

This newsletter has discussed a wide variety of subjects over the past three years. These newsletters are not necessarily intellectually stimulating nor do I sense any particular expression of theological acumen. The purpose of these newsletters is to awaken the sleeping giants in the evangelical church before it is too late and to serve as a format for discussion. This issue discusses the assessment centers that have become popular in recent years among different Presbyterian denominations.

A long time ago, in fact over one hundred and fifty years ago, James Henley Thornwell warned the Presbyterian church of the dangers of church boards. In his Argument against Church-Boards Thornwell said, "All reformations are gradual. The evils of ancient abuses do not develop themselves at once. The light breaks in upon the mind slowly and feebly at first, like the first beams of morning, and, like them, also waxes stronger and stronger until all darkness is dissipated and the hidden things of dishonesty are openly revealed." He is so correct. We churchmen (sinners that we are) regress theologically. Theological regression is evident by the use of assessment centers. These centers have established a dogma for church planting that is administrated by managerial and therapeutic theories from the world of business and psychology. The opportunistic secularism found in corporate management and psychological therapeutics continues to gain favor in denominational agencies. These unbiblical innovative ideas, such as assessment centers, hinder the biblical innovative ideas such as theological integrity, sound worship practices, and family worship.

Men and men alone should be able to offer evidence to the Presbytery (the only judicatory authorized to ordain ministers of the gospel) that God's call for them is one of an evangelist. I've devoted nearly five years to the research of the church growth movement. The purpose of this book is not to critique the church growth movement. A critique has already been published under the title *The god of the Church Growth Movement* and may be obtained from Greenville Presbyterian Theological Seminary. My point is that I've heard all the arguments for church growth movement methodology from their own advocates and the assessment center has grown out of the church growth movement. We cannot understand the assessment center concept unless we understand the church growth movement philosophy.

In July 1990, I attended the Saddlebrook Conference sponsored by the Presbyterian Church in America. It was a week-long conference for ministers and their wives who planned to start a new church. They had church growth experts on hand to teach the concepts that would produce results. These were all "successful church planters" or either professionals in the field of church growth even though they hadn't successfully planted a church, such as Mr. Tom Hawkes. During that week I tried to be open minded and objective. However, the psychological testing was first of all worthless and second it was unbiblical. The proponents of managerialism were manifestly more interested in methodology than in theological integrity. The grand finale that set me on my current research course was a statement made by the seminar leader that spoke on "preaching." This successful church planter (successful as in his individual church plant and the number of churches he had supported financially as church plants) said "you have to learn to communicate truth without people knowing it." If you think this church growth expert is confused, just think of the thousands of people he has tried to deceive over the years! It is impossible to know truth without knowing it.

There are certain phrases used by the proponents of assessment centers. "Successful church planters" is one of those important aphorisms. I note that some even say "successful church planters and their wives." It is serious fundamental fallacious argumentation to make the statement that a man and his wife can successfully start a church based on any previous success. Does it mean that he can successfully start another church? I think it is a mistake to look at fallible individuals, except the Lord Jesus Himself who is infallible, for examples of success. But for the sake of argument I'll grant we should look at successful church planters. The apostle Paul was a successful church planter, par excellence, yet he was not successful in every effort. If we are talking about McDonalds there is predictable certainty in success, but not so with the church. The assumption is that the concepts are easily transferable from location to location and from person to person. Multilevel marketing companies have used this concept for years. It not only is a fallacious argument, it is dangerous to idolize other "successful church planters." Now why are the wives involved? If you serve in a denomination that ordains women ministers, then some women should be involved in the assessment center. However, if women are not ordained ministers, why should they be tested for their gifts, because they are not evangelists.

Another phrase that surfaces is "evaluate the candidates' gifts for church planting." What gifts are in mind? I've heard terms like spiritual maturity, leadership, planning skills, evangelism and disciple skills, martial relationship, et al, as the desired gifts for church planting. If these areas must come under scrutiny, and they should, then the Bible must be our guide to determine the presence or lack of these gifts. The Bible lists the qualifications for elders in 1 Timothy 3:1-7 and it seems that all those qualities are moral except one – the ability to teach. Why not have the Presbytery, the proper body according to Presbyterian church government, conduct the assessment based on the criteria in 1 Timothy? If any models are used, they should be biblical models used by men like the apostle Paul or better yet the Lord Jesus Christ. But then their approach was not very popular. The Bible never records that our Lord Jesus Christ ever laughed, He didn't cater to religious leaders, but He did have a passion for truth. His earthly ministry produced the greatest reformation the church has ever known, even without an assessment center. The preaching of the Lord Jesus Christ was "hard teaching" and "many turned back and no longer followed him" (John 6:60ff). Are we so naive as to believe that the stamp of approval by an assessment center will send out a man who can turn "hard teaching" into easy teaching and bring many in who would not follow the Lord?

Assessment centers are at the core unbiblical. Under the heading "The Value of Assessments Centers" published in The ARP Magazine in January 1994 asserted that "assessments are both Biblical and Presbyterian." The proof texts given were 1 Timothy 3, Titus 1, and 1 Timothy 5:22 which are not proof texts for assessment centers. The first two are primarily evidences (proof texts) for elder qualifications and the last one has to do with ordination. All of this (determine qualifications and ordain men) is the job of presbytery, not the job of a denominational office.

The writer is correct to say that Presbyterian churches have traditionally assessed ministerial candidates. I'll grant the possibility that assessment centers are needed, but presbytery must assess the candidate. Unfortunately Presbyterians too often act like Congregationalists rather than Presbyterians. They hire people to do the job that presbyters will not do. Soon the bureaucracy is at work. Huge salaries are paid to guarantee the certainty of results. Assessment centers then become the means to an end.

Assessment centers at the core are not biblical or Presbyterian. They advocate methods and concepts that are not in keeping with confessional standards. They are a threat to doctrinal integrity. We must be distinctively Reformed in our convictions, our methods, and our testimony. We must remember it is the Holy Spirit adding to our number. It is our job to testify of God's grace according to the Scriptures. Thornwell is right. Reformations are gradual.

Appendix B

Originally published in the theological newsletter, *Informed and Reformed*, October 1996

Does anybody know where our Reformed churches are going? When Alice in Wonderland asked the cat where she ought to go the cat said "That depends a good deal on where you want to get to." Now back to my original question: Does anybody know where our Reformed churches want to get to?

God commissioned Joshua to plant the twelve tribes of Israel, the church of the Old Testament, in an area without the approval of the demographic experts and without the assistance of a "flagship" tribe (church). Joshua was not told to go to the church planting center for a seminar or the assessment center for an assessment. He was not told to listen to the experts in the field of sociology, psychology, or management experts. Joshua's instruction may be summed up in these few words: "Only be strong and very courageous, that you may observe to do according to all the law which Moses My servant commanded you; do not turn from it to the right hand or to the left, that you may prosper wherever you go. This Book of the Law shall not depart from your mouth, but you shall meditate in it day and night, that you may observe to do according to all that is written in it" (Joshua 1:7-8).

Sylvester Stallone was the protagonist in the movie "Lockup." He was unjustly imprisoned, so he tried to escape.

During the escape, his partner told Stallone to turn left, but Stallone argued that he should turn right. At his partner's insistence, Stallone turned left and the prison guards captured him. It turned out that his partner betrayed him and was an informer for the prison officials. Making the wrong turn can be very painful or bring death itself. Is it possible that many professing Reformed ministers and ruling elders have taken the wrong turn in church leadership? Is it possible that the spirit of this modern/postmodern world has deceived Reformed ministers and ruling elders? Is it possible to discuss these possibilities? I think the answer to all three of those questions is "yes!"

There are, to my mind, many professing Reformed ministers and ruling elders who have taken a wrong turn in church leadership. The evidence demands a verdict. The evidence is that more and more professing Reformed churches have adopted the methods of the church growth movement. Notice I said methods, because the church growth movement has no definitive theological system. I made that comment in a paper Dr. Michael Horton reviewed and he quickly pointed out that they do have a theological system. Are they not all Arminian in their evangelistic views? I've never known a church that adopted the methodology of the church growth movement that didn't employ eclectic worship practices. Their lack of theology drives them to pragmatism. Their pragmatism drives them toward man-centered authority and away from God-centered authority in matters of faith and practice.

The advocates of the church growth movement have agendas that are incongruous with what the Puritans called the regulative principle and what we call a Reformed world and life view. I could cite numerous examples, but one will suffice. I have before me a report from a mission church that boasts of its women's ministry, Promise Keepers involvement, children's church, small group dynamics, and drama team. I smell anti-covenant theology, Arminianism, inadequate elder leadership, and flagrant violations of scriptural principles in worship in such boasting. In the four page report one whole page is given to "church growth patterns" which is a statistical report about increases in membership and money. If the word church was removed, it would appear that it was no more than a progress report of any secular entrepreneurial enterprise. The goal is success and success is in numbers. Success in this case is the development of unbiblical programs and using doctrinal principles that are opposite of those in the confession used by that particular denomination.

The arguments in favor of the pragmatic methods tend to focus on stewardship. The advocates tell us that "God requires good stewardship." Therefore, prudence dictates the consultation of management experts to get the most for your money. Biblical stewardship is married to good sound management, but biblical stewardship follows from faithfulness. Faithfulness is what God had in mind when He sent Joshua in the land of Canaan. Joshua didn't have the option of hiring the Egyptian Army to do his fighting. Joshua had to do it God's way and nothing else was acceptable.

The church growth movement has turned from God's regulative principle. Denominational leaders and financiers actively promote the church growth movement through denominational and independent seminaries. The watershed effect finds its way to pastors who are constantly challenged by local church leaders and congregations to grow, grow, grow. The pastor sees the glitter and gold. He needs an increase in salary, so why not employ these church growth movement methods. The pastor probably thinks "it's not that big of a compromise and who would be against church growth." No Christian can be opposed to church growth, but all Christians must be opposed to church growth methodology that is not in keeping with the Word of God. Compromise is dangerous because the uncritical thinker assumes that God will not require obedience. Dr. Os Guinness reminds us that "[C]ompromise is compromise regardless of when, how, or why it happens. . . ."

The wrong turn to the methods of the church growth movement began at the top with church leadership. Sometimes it seems so right to make the wrong turn. "We should therefore heed Origin's ancient principle: Christians are free to plunder the Egyptians, but forbidden to set up a golden calf" (Dining With the Devil, p. 90).

Christians seem to be so easily diverted to the right or to the left. I think it is the spirit of this modern/postmodern world. It doesn't matter which world you live in, they both have seductive powers that are equally dangerous. The end of each system denies the authority and sovereignty of God.

Modernity depends on the inherent ability of rationalism to conquer the world with modernism through industry, technology and telecommunications. Postmodernity reduces intelligent human discourse to an irrational vacuum supported only by the feeling of personal interpretation. It stands to reason that if a church planter uses the right laws of management, understands psychological needs, embraces the pietistic practices of Christianity, and makes a vow to a creed or confession that can be interpreted relative to purpose, then surely he will be successful and please God at the same time. And after all, look at what the church planter has done for God! The temptation to follow the ways of the world is very tempting indeed. So many diversions are before God's people. The dangers of idolatry are ever present. Therefore, I think it is possible for Reformed leaders and laymen to embrace the church growth movement. But I also think it is possible for God to show them the error of their ways.

It doesn't take a precocious genius to realize that the language of the Bible simply doesn't square with the language of the church growth movement experts. It doesn't take an intellectual giant to realize that a "user-friendly church" is nothing more than the *argumentum ad populum*. This argument simply appeals to public opinion. God's Word will not change even if 100% of the people vote against Him. You don't have to be a scholar to realize that church growth movement churches keep their sermons brief and humorous. Anecdotal preaching reduces the sermon to a talk that ultimately entertains. You don't have to look very far to see the anti-intellectual agenda in the church growth movement.

The starting point for these discussions is the Puritan regulative principle. The Word of God must be the determining principle for any Christian belief system and the method that follows from that belief system. The church growth movement advocates must meet at the debate table willing to engage in fruitful discussion that will lead to reformation (discovery or rediscovery) of biblical truth.

The primary duty of converted souls is to offer to the God of our salvation God-centered worship. During the concourse of worship the law and the gospel goes forth and something happens when a soul hears the preaching of the Word of God (see 2 Corinthians 2:12-17). All the programs, all the man-centered ideas, all the managerial expertise, and all the psychological strategies will never change God's plan for planting churches. The glitter, gold, and glib tongue of the church growth movement may be the popular method to plant churches, but God's people, gracious patience, and genuine preaching is the God-centered way to plant churches.

End Notes

[1] Jonathan Edwards, *The Works of Jonathan Edwards*. Vol. 1: Memoirs of Jonathan Edwards. Carlisle, Penn.: The Banner of Truth Trust, 1974, p. xxxi.

[2] John G. Gerstner, *The Rational Biblical Theology of Jonathan* Edwards, vol. 2, (Berea Publications: Powhatan, Virginia and Ligonier Ministries: Orlando, Fla, 1992), p. 125.

[3] David Wells, *No Place for Truth*, (William B. Eerdmans Publishing Co., 1993), p. 4.

[4] Os Guinness, *The American Hour*, (New York: The Free Press, 1993) p. 26.

[5] David Wells, *No Place For Truth*, p. 72.

[6] Ibid, p. 7

[7] Michael Horton, *Made in America*, (Grand Rapids: Baker Book House, 1991). p. 16.

[8] Alasdair MacIntyre, *After Virtue*, (Notre Dame: University of Notre Dame Press, 1981), p. 77.

[9] J. Gresham Machen, *Christianity and Liberalism*, (Grand Rapids: William B. Eerdmans Publishing Company, 1923). p. 5,6.

[10] James Davison Hunter, *Culture Wars*, (n.p. Basic Books, A Division of HarperCollins Publishers, 1991). p. 63.

[11] Os Guinness and John Seel, *No God But God*, (Chicago: Moody Press, 1992), p. 95.

[12] Alasdair MacIntyre, *After Virtue*, p. 77.

[13] Guinness and Seel, *No God But God*, p. 148.

[14] Os Guinness, *Dining With the Devil*, (Grand Rapids: Baker Book House, 1993), p. 31.

[15] Ibid., p. 31.

[16] David Wells, *No Place for Truth*, p. 61.

[17] Gene Veith, Jr, *Postmodern Times*, (Wheaton, Ill.: Crossway Books, 1994), p. 51

[18] Thomas C. Oden, *After Modernity. . .What?*, (Grand Rapids: Zondervan Publishing House, 1990), p. 80.

[19] Ibid., p. 46.

[20] Herbert Schlossberg, *Idols For Destruction*, (Washington D. C.: Regnery Gateway, 1990), p. 36, 37.

[21] David Wells, *No Place for Truth*, p. 104.

[22] Kenneth A. Myers, *All God's Children and Blue Suede Shoes*, (Wheaton, Ill.: Crossway Books, 1989), p. 108.

[23] Thomas Oden, *After Modernity. . .What?*, p. 52.

[24] David Wells, *No Place for Truth*, p. 101.

[25] Michael Scott Horton, *Made in America*, p. 44.

[26] Ibid, p. 12

[27] Ibid.

[28] James Davison Hunter, *Culture Wars*, p. 138.

[29] Donald A. McGavran, *How to Grow a Church*, (Glendale, Calif.: Regal Books Division, G/L Publications, 1973), p. 79

[30] Lee Roy Taylor, Jr., *A Flagship Church Planting Strategy for the Presbyterian Church in America*, (Ann Arbor,

Mich.: U.M.I. Dissertation Information Service, 1991), p. 33.

[31] Terry L. Gyger, Dave B. Calhoun, and E. Walford Thompson, *Handbook for Church Growth*, (Coral Gables, Fla.: Ministries In Action, 1983), p. 223-225.

[32] Michael G. Maudlin and Edward Gilbreath, *Selling Out the House of God*, Christianity Today, June 18, 1994, p.23.

[33] Win Arn, *The Pastor's Church Growth Handbook*, (Pasadena, Calif.: Church Growth Press, 1982), p. 87.

[34] George Barna, *Marketing The Church*, (Colorado Springs, Colo.: Navpress, 1989) p.14.

[35] C. Wayne Zunkel, *Church Growth Under Fire*, (Scottdale, Penn.: Herald Press, 1987) p. 218.

[36] Foster H. Shannon, *The Growth Crisis in the American Church*, (South Pasadena, Calif.: William Carey Library, 1977) p. 3.

[37] Donald A McGavran, *How to Grow a Church*, p. 79

[38] J. Robertson McQuilkin, *Measuring the Church Growth Movement*, (Chicago: Moody Press, 1973), p. 76.

[39] Ibid., p. 12

[40] Ibid., p. 13.
[41] Ibid., p. 24

[42] C. Peter Wagner, *Church Growth and the Whole Gospel*, (San Francisco: Harper and Row Publishers, 1981) p. 57.

[43] Lee Roy Taylor, Jr., *A Flagship church Planting Strategy for the Presbyterian Church in America*, p. 111.

[44] Michael Horton, *Beyond Culture Wars*, (Chicago: Moody Press, 1994), p. 63

[45] Ken Sidey, "Church Growth Fine Tunes Its Formulas," Christianity Today, June 24, 1991, p.44.

[46] R. C. Sproul, *Lifeviews*, (Old Tappan, New Jersey: Fleming H. Revell Co., 1986), p. 77.

[47] C. Peter Wagner, *Church Growth State of the Art*, (Wheaton: Tyndale House, 1986), p. 290.

[48] Douglas Webster, *Selling Jesus*, (Downers Grove, Ill.: Intervarsity Press, 1992), p. 75

[49] Ken Sidney, "Church Growth Fine Tunes Its Formulas," p. 45.

[50] Lee Roy Taylor, Jr., *A Flagship church Planting Strategy for the Presbyterian Church in America*, p. 111.

[51] Douglas Webster, *Selling Jesus*, p. 58

[52] Terry L. Gyger, Dave B. Calhoun, and E. Walford Thompson, *Handbook For Church Growth*, p. 271

[53] Michael Horton, *Beyond Culture Wars*, p. 109.

[54] Ibid.

[55] Michael Scott Horton, *Made In America*, p. 49.

[56] Os Guinness, *Dining With The Devil*, p. 25.

[57] Douglas Webster, *Selling Jesus*, p. 111.

[58] Michael Scott Horton, *Made In America*, p. 71.

[59] Os Guinness, *Dining With The Devil*, p. 58

[60] Ibid., p. 65

[61] Rev. David Coffin, "Letters to the Editor," Christianity Today, August 19, 1991, p. 5.

[62] Frank R. Tillapaugh, *Unleashing the Church*, (Ventura, Calif.: Regal Books, 1982), p. 32.

[63] John Calvin, *Institutes of the Christian Religion*, ed. John T. McNeill vol. 2 (Philadelphia: The Westminster Press, 1960, p. 1024.

[64] J. Gresham Machen, *Education, Christianity, and the State*, (Jefferson, Maryland: The Trinity Foundation, 1987), p. 8.

[65] Brian A. Bernal, "The Power of the Word Preached," The Banner of Truth, March 1994, p. 22.

[66] Robert L. Dabney, *Sacred Rhetoric*, (Carlisle, Penn.: The Banner of Truth Trust, 1979) p. 37.

[67] Douglas Webster, *Selling Jesus*, p. 107.

[68] Thomas C. Oden, *After Modernity. . .What?*, p. 31

[69] C. Peter Wagner, *Church Growth and the Whole Gospel*, p. 83.

[70] Michael Horton, *Beyond Culture Wars*, p. 67.

[71] Donald McGavran and George G. Hunter III, *Church Growth Strategies that Work*, (Nashville: Abingdon, 1980) p. 19

[72] Os Guinness, *Dining With the Devil*, p. 75

[73] David Wells, *No Place For Truth*, p. 280.

[74]Matthew 6:24 (New American Standard Version)

[75]Thomas C. Oden, *After Modernity. . .What?*, p. 151.

[76]Jitsuo Moridawa, *Biblical Dimensions of Church Growth*, (Valley Forge, Pa.:   Judson Press, 1979), p.46

About the Author

Martin Murphy has a B.A. in Bible from Columbia International University and Master of Divinity from Reformed Theological Seminary. Martin spent nearly thirty years in the class room, the pulpit, the lectern, the study, and the library. He now devotes most of his time consolidating academic and practical gains by writing books. He and his wife Mary live in Dothan, Alabama. He is the author of twelve Christian books.

The Church: First Thirty Years, 344 pages, ISBN 9780985618179, $15.95. This book is an exposition of the Book of Acts. It will help Christians understand the purpose, mission, and ministry of the church.

The Dominant Culture: Living in the Promised Land, 172 pages, ISBN 970991481118, $11.95. This book examines the culture of Israel during the period of the Judges. It explains how worldviews influence the church and it reveals biblical principles to help Christians learn how to live in the culture.

My Christian Apology, 98 pages, ISBN 9780984570874, $7.95. This book investigates the doctrine of Christian apologetics. It explains rational Christian apologetics.

The Essence of Christian Doctrine, 200 pages, ISBN 9780984570812, $12.95. This book was written so that pastors and laymen would have a quick reference to major biblical doctrines. Dr. Steve Brown says it was written, "with clarity and power about the verities of the Christian faith and in a way that makes a difference in how we live."

Return to the Lord, 130 pages, ISBN 9780984570805, $8.95. This book is an exposition of Hosea. The prophet speaks a message of repentance and hope. Hosea's prophetic message to Old Testament and New Testament congregations is, "you have broken God's covenant; return to the Lord." Dr. Richard Pratt said, "We need more correct and practical instruction in the prophetic books, and you have given us just that."

Theological Terms in Layman Language, 130 pages, ISBN 9780985618155, $8.95. This book was written so that simple words like faith or not so simple words like aseity are explained in plain language. Theological Terms in Layman Language is easy to read and designed for people who want a brief definition for theological terms. The terms are in layman friendly language.

Brief Study of the Ten Commandments, 164 pages, 9780991481163, $10.95. This book will help Christians discover or re-discover the meaning of the Ten Commandments.

The Present Truth, 164 pages, ISBN 9780983244172, $8.95. Each chapter examines a topic relative to the Christian life. Topics such as church, sin, anger, marriage, education and more.

Doctrine of Sound Words: Summary of Christian Theology, 423 pages, ISBN 9780991481125, $16.95. This is a book of Christian doctrine in topical format. It covers a wide range of theological topics such as, the triune God, creation, providence, sin, justification, repentance, Christian liberty, free will, marriage and divorce, Christian fellowship, et al). There are thirty three topics beginning with "Holy Scriptures" and ending with "The Last Judgment." It is a systematic theology for laymen based on the full counsel of God.

Friendship: The Joy of Relationships, ISBN 9780986405518, 48 pages, $6.49. This is the kind of book that friends give each other and share the principles with each other. If friends do not feel comfortable sharing these relationship principles with each other, the friendship may not really exist. Friendship involves a relationship of distinction. It is a relationship that respects the dignity of another person. The Bible teaches a different version of what it means to be a friend than the popular culture teaches. There are many occasions when friends say they are friends, but they are not friends. "Even my own familiar friend in whom I trusted, who ate my bread, has lifted up his heel against me" (Psalm 41:9). A true friend will endure and sacrifice for a friend. "A friend loves at all times" (Proverbs 17:7) and "there is a friend who sticks closer than a brother" (Proverbs 18:24).

Ultimate Authority for the Soul, ISBN 9780986405501, 151 pages, $9.99. What is the ultimate authority for human beings? This book examines that question and concludes that every rational being has some recognition of God as the ultimate authority. Although God is the ultimate authority, He confers His authority by means of the Word of God. The author examines Psalm 119 to build a defense for the ultimate authority for the soul. Although this book was written for Christians, the author builds the case that authority is a principle necessary to maintain sanity and order in the family, the church and civil society. The Word of God connects the soul with reality.

www.ingramcontent.com/pod-product-compliance
Lightning Source LLC
Chambersburg PA
CBHW070549030426
42337CB00016B/2420